The Fall of Two Houses

THE FALL OF TWO HOUSES

A Play

A Sequel to Romeo and Juliet

Written by Rudolph Ortiz

Licensing & Contact

For performance rights or production inquiries, please contact: Rudolph Ortiz

Email: Rudymx13@gmail.com

Website or Portfolio: @rudymx13

This script is an original dramatic work inspired by characters and themes from William Shakespeare's *Romeo and Juliet* (public domain). All original text, structure, and character development are the intellectual property of the author.

The Fall of Two Houses: A Sequel to Romeo and Juliet

This is an original dramatic work inspired by William Shakespeare's *Romeo and Juliet*, which is in the public domain. All original scenes, characters, dialogue, and thematic development in this edition are the intellectual property of the author.

For performance rights, licensing, or reproduction inquiries, please contact:

Rudolph Ortiz

Rudymx13@gmail.com

First Edition: 2025

Printed in the United States of America

ISBN: 979-8-9987548-0-7

Table of Contents

Dedication

For my wife, my family, and all those who believe in me—and even those who don't.

Thank you for being part of the fire that forged this story.

Author's Note

This story began with a question: What happens after the curtain falls? I wanted to explore not just the tragedy of Romeo and Juliet—but the scars left behind. What happens to the people who survive love, war, silence, and failure? Who tells their story?

Rosaline was never given a voice in Shakespeare's play. Here, she becomes the soul of the city—a woman shaped by loss who ultimately chooses quiet devotion over power. Every character in this play walks through fire—some are consumed by it, and some rise through the ash.

This is not a love story. It is the aftermath of one.

— Rudolph Ortiz

Performance Notes for Directors

Tone & Setting: This is not a romantic play—it is a post-tragedy, with the tone of loss, ruin, and painful reflection. Every act should feel like the echo of a past explosion. Use ash, ruin, and silence visually to carry the emotional weight.

Lighting: Favor dim, naturalistic lighting—torchlight, candlelight, sunrise glows. Ash and shadows should dominate the first three acts, shifting to golden sunrise hues only in Act V.

Sound Design: Avoid grand scores. Instead, use minimal atmospheric sound—faint bells, wind, distant fire crackle, and silences. When music appears (like during the epilogue), let it be humble and human— something played by strings or children.

Ghosts: When Romeo and Juliet appear in Act V, Scene 1, they should be luminous but not spectral. They don't speak. Their presence should feel like closure, not horror.

Rosaline: She is the soul of the play. Her emotional arc should be restrained until Act IV. Her silence at the end is louder than any cry. Let her final scene feel peaceful, not tragic.

The Child: The future. Let this role be played with sincerity and clarity. His writing scenes are sacred. Avoid overly sentimental staging—focus on calm wonder and resolve.

Doubling Roles: Ensemble members can play guards, mourners, rioters, and ghosts. The feeling should be of a city crumbling inward, then slowly rebuilding through shared memory.

Final Line Echo: When "Two households, both alike in dignity..." is recited at the end, it should feel like a legend retold—not a prophecy fulfilled. A whisper across generations.

Costume Design: Garments should reflect decay, mourning, and humility. Use earth tones, ash-stained fabric, and distressed materials. Nobles wear faded richness—once-glorious silks, now torn or soot-marked. Commoners wear rough linen. Rosaline transitions from noble darks to neutral robes. By Act V, the child wears cleaner, simpler cloth to symbolize renewal.

Music Suggestions: Use live or ambient strings—cello, viola, and sparse piano. Avoid swelling orchestral pieces. Let scenes breathe in silence. For key moments (the funeral, the reading, the orchard), consider solo instrumental music—something that echoes grief but leaves space for reflection. Final notes should fade like memory, not crash like climax.

Prologue: Before the Ashes: Stage this scene as a memory—slow, minimal, and ghostlike. Use dim lighting, no music, and soft, deliberate movement. Romeo and Juliet should feel like echoes caught in time. Their final pose—hands touching—must visually mirror the way they're later found in The Night Funeral. The Prince's voice should be faint, as if whispered through history.

Props: Use minimal, symbolic props. A bloodied crest, a scorched ribbon, a family seal, or Juliet's heirloom can carry emotional resonance. Books, scrolls, and parchment should be present in most scenes involving the child or Rosaline.

Scene Transitions: Between scenes, dim the lights slowly and use sparse musical cues (such as a single cello note or soft bell toll). Avoid blackouts until act breaks. Let transitions feel like breathing—the calm between storms.

Printing/Production Note: For staging in minimalist sets, consider background projections for Verona's skyline or chapel ruins, allowing fluid shifts between scenes. Use one rotating platform if available to keep action dynamic.

List of Acts and Scenes

PROLOGUE: Before the Ashes

Romeo and Juliet's deaths are shown in silence—soft, haunting, and inevitable. Romeo drinks the poison. Juliet wakes too late. She kisses him, finds no warmth, and takes her own life with his dagger. Their hands fall together. The Prince's voice echoes: "All are punished."
This memory sets the tone for what follows—the world after love has died.

ACT I: The Day After Love Died

Scene 1: After the Blood

The PRINCE of Verona addresses the city after the deaths of Romeo and Juliet. Tybalt's uncle and Mercutio's brother stir up the crowd, calling for revenge. Riots begin. The PRINCE bans blood feuds and house banners. But Verona is already fracturing.

Scene 2: A Silence Too Heavy

Inside the Capulet estate, Lady Capulet confronts Juliet's nurse, who confesses to helping Juliet secretly marry Romeo. Overwhelmed with guilt, the nurse takes her own life. As Lady Capulet grieves, rioters breach the estate. Fire spreads.

Scene 3: The Collapse of Montague

At the Montague estate, Lady Montague has died from grief over Romeo's exile. Lord Montague stands hollowed but upright. With the house falling around him, he prepares to flee with a retainer, taking only what he can carry. Benvolio stays behind to witness the fall.

Scene 4: The Mob Devours Itself

Tybalt's uncle and Mercutio's brother ignite a street duel between their factions. Both men kill each other. The mob, disillusioned, turns on itself. Fires erupt across Verona. The houses crumble. Act I ends in flames.

ACT II: Embers of the Past

Scene 1: Beneath the Chapel

Friar Laurence prepares Romeo and Juliet's bodies for burial in a crypt. Lord Montague arrives in secret, worn and quiet. Lord Capulet, wounded, also arrives. He weeps beside Juliet. The Friar gives a funeral prayer. As Lord Montague turns to speak to him, he discovers Capulet has died silently beside his daughter.

Scene 2: Rosaline Among Ruins

Rosaline, sitting in the remains of a garden, speaks with a boy about Romeo and Juliet. She reflects on love, war, and silence. Friar Laurence finds her there. They speak of truth, guilt, and legacy. Rosaline agrees: the story must be told.

Scene 3: The Last Montague

Benvolio, the final member of House Montague, prepares to leave the city. He leaves the family crest behind. An old priest advises him to flee or die. Benvolio exits into the unknown, saying, "Let the last Montague walk away from the fire."

Scene 4: The People Speak

Citizens gather in the marketplace. The old apothecary admits he sold Romeo the poison. People begin piling the dead, regardless of side. The child mimics the war, then lays down his sword. The crowd begins to listen.

ACT III: Inferno

Scene 1: Fire in the House of Capulet

Lady Capulet tries to save a memory of Juliet but is surrounded by rioters and fire. She chooses not to flee and walks into the flames as the estate collapses.

Scene 2: The Night Funeral

In the crypt, Friar Laurence arranges the joint burial of Romeo and Juliet. Lord Montague mourns his son. Lord Capulet dies from his wounds. A young servant delivers Lady Capulet's scorched heirloom to Juliet's side. Lord Montague offers a final prayer and disappears into the night with only a small satchel.

Scene 3: The Confession

Friar Laurence writes a full confession of his role in Romeo and Juliet's deaths. He leaves the letter beside Juliet and removes his robes. He walks into the dawn, no longer a priest—only a man who failed to save them.

Scene 4: Too Late

Friar John finds the confession too late. Drunk and broken, he gives the letter to Rosaline. She chooses to take the truth and share it.

ACT IV: Ashes of Verona

Scene 1: The Telling

In the marketplace, Rosaline speaks to the remaining citizens. She tells the true story of Romeo and Juliet—not as a romantic tragedy, but as a warning. People bury the dead, regardless of name. A young boy begins writing their tale.

Scene 2: The Letter

Rosaline finds Friar Laurence's confession in the crypt. She confronts Friar John, still drunk with guilt. She contemplates whether to share the truth or let the myth survive. She chooses truth, and takes the letter.

Scene 3: The Monument

In the city square, Rosaline reads the letter to the public. There are no protests, no violence—only silence and understanding. The boy gives her his written version of the story. A sense of fragile hope returns to the city.

Scene 4: A Quiet Vow

In the early morning, Rosaline walks alone through the remains of the Capulet chapel. She finds a group of nuns clearing debris and planting herbs in what was once a courtyard.

ACT V: Ghosts of Verona

Scene 1: The Orchard

Time has passed. The boy sits beneath a tree, writing Romeo and Juliet's story. He leaves the book near a small stone marked "R + J." As he exits, ghostly figures of Romeo and Juliet appear. They hold hands and look out over Verona. The sun rises. Final peace. He becomes Luigi da Porto—the man who will preserve the tale that one day inspires Shakespeare.

EPILOGUE

The Scholar's Room

Years later, the boy—now an old man—writes quietly in a study filled with books. A new child enters, asking if the story was true. The scholar nods and begins to tell it once more, ensuring the truth is passed on. History becomes memory. And the memory lives on.

THE END.

Dramatis Personae

😷 The Families

- **Romeo Montague** – Son of the Montague house; dies by poison beside Juliet.
- **Juliet Capulet** – Daughter of the Capulet house; dies by dagger beside Romeo.
- **Lord Montague:**Attends the funeral and subsequently flees the city.
- **Lady Montague:** Dies from grief after Romeo's exile.
- **Lord Capulet** – Juliet's father; mortally wounded and dies at the funeral.
- **Lady Capulet** – Juliet's mother; perishes in a house fire started during the riot.

⚔ The Conflict

- **Tybalt** – Juliet's cousin; deceased before the play begins, but his family stirs the war.
- **Mercutio** – Romeo's close friend; his death fuels the brewing violence.
- **Benvolio** – Romeo's cousin; leaves Verona in sorrow and never finds closure.
- **Paris** – Juliet's suitor; dies in the early chaos of the civil war.

😊 The Faith

- **Friar Laurence** – Priest who secretly marries Romeo and Juliet; writes a confession and abandons his post.
- **Friar John** – Fails to deliver the letter that could've saved the lovers; drinks himself into guilt and gives the confession to Rosaline.

✳️ The Observers

- **Rosaline** – Juliet's cousin and Romeo's former love; survives to tell the true story to the people of Verona.
- **Balthasar** – Romeo's servant; brings Romeo's dagger to the funeral.
- **Juliet's Nurse** – Dies by suicide from guilt for helping the secret marriage.

👥 The People of Verona

- **Fishmonger** – A grieving citizen who lost his sons to the feud.
- **Midwife** – Delivered Juliet at birth; helps bury the dead after the war.
- **Old Man** – The apothecary who sold poison to Romeo; lost everything in the fire.
- **Young Servant** – Tried to save Lady Capulet; brings her burned keepsake to Juliet's tomb.
- **Child** – Witness to the tragedy; becomes a writer who records the truth.
- **New Child** – Appears in the epilogue; receives the story from the now-aged writer.
- **Prince Escalus** – Ruler of Verona. He seeks peace after the lovers' death, attempts to rebuild the city, and ultimately steps down to let the people govern themselves.

PROLOGUE

Before the Ashes

Scene: The Capulet tomb. Dim, echoing. The world holds its breath.

JULIET lies motionless on the bier, the empty vial of potion in her hand. Enter ***ROMEO****, breathless, dirt-smudged, holding the poison.*

ROMEO (kneeling beside her):

Here lies my heart's light... extinguished.
Not banished—buried.
Here's to love, undelivered.
He drinks the poison. Staggers. Falls beside her.

*A moment later, **Juliet stirs**. Her eyes flutter open. She sees Romeo—his lips blue, his breath gone. Her scream is soundless.*

JULIET (barely whispering):

Why... why did you not wait?

She kisses his lips, hoping for poison.

JULIET:

No warm breath. No heartbeat.
Then there's no world left.

She finds his dagger. Without hesitation, she drives it into her chest and collapses beside him. Their hands fall together—touching.

The scene holds still.

A candle snuffs out. The tomb darkens. And from the silence, the voice of the **PRINCE** *echoes—faint, like memory:*

PRINCE (voiceover):

All are punished.

BLACKOUT.

ACT I

ACT I

The Day After Love Died

Scene 1: After the Blood

Scene: The central square of Verona. Ash drifts through the air. The remains of a torn Capulet banner hang from a statue. A crowd gathers—nervous, angry, fractured. Soldiers stand guard along the perimeter. The PRINCE of Verona stands atop a platform, flanked by guards.

PRINCE:

Citizens of Verona—hear me now.
Two children—Romeo Montague and Juliet Capulet—lie cold beneath the altar.
Not from plague. Not from fate.
From us.

The crowd murmurs. Some weep. Others scowl.

PRINCE (cont'd):

I have seen your grief. I have seen your rage.
But I will not let this city fall for the sins of its houses.
From this day forward—
No banners. No vendettas. No blood in the name of Montague or Capulet.

A voice interrupts from the crowd.

TYBALT'S UNCLE (shouting):

They murdered Tybalt!
And now they mourn the boy who spilled his blood?

MERCUTIO'S BROTHER (pushing forward):

And what of Mercutio?
Dead in the street like a dog while nobles weep over lovers?

Both men step forward, flanked by their factions—riot-worn, armed citizens with scraps of noble crests.

TYBALT'S UNCLE:

We call for justice.

MERCUTIO'S BROTHER:

We call for reckoning.

PRINCE (shouting):

You call for ruin!
You bury children with your pride!

A tense silence—broken by distant screaming and a column of smoke rising behind the buildings.

Enter PARIS, bruised and limping, pushing through the crowd toward the platform. His once-noble clothes are torn, bloodied. His sword is already drawn. His eyes are wild with grief

PARIS:

Enough! Is there no one left who will honor the dead without stoking the fire?
Juliet is gone. Romeo is gone. Must you drown their memory in more blood?

TYBALT'S UNCLE:

You dare speak of honor? You, who would have married her under her father's lies?

PARIS:

But she died before I could... and I—
He falters
—I found her cold, already in the tomb.
I held her hand. I begged her to wake.
And when she didn't...
he swallows hard
...I stayed beside her until the city turned its back on all of us.

MERCUTIO'S BROTHER:

Then die with her, noble fool!

He lunges, but guards hold him back. The crowd surges. The square begins to collapse into violence.

PRINCE:

Hold! Stop this—!
Enter a MESSENGER, blood on his sleeves.

MESSENGER (shouting):

The Capulet chapel has been stormed!
Paris... Paris was found there—kneeling beside Juliet's tomb.
He survived his duel with Romeo.
He drew his blade on the mob.
They cut him down.
Paris is dead!

A stunned silence. Then—

TYBALT'S UNCLE (to his men):

Then we meet them with fire!

MERCUTIO'S BROTHER (drawing sword):

For Mercutio!

They clash. Chaos erupts. The crowd breaks into factions. The guards cannot contain the surge.

TYBALT'S UNCLE and MERCUTIO'S BROTHER fight viciously—wounded, bloodied. At the climax, they kill each other in a final blow—both collapsing in the dust.

A CITIZEN stares at the bodies, stunned.

CITIZEN:

They're dead... both of them.

ANOTHER CITIZEN:

Then who's left to lead us?

Smoke thickens. Screams rise. Swords clash. The square dissolves into civil war.

BLACKOUT.

Scene 2: A Silence Too Heavy

Scene: A dim corridor in the Capulet estate. Tapestries torn, furniture overturned. Candles burn low. Outside the windows, smoke drifts through the sky. Distant shouting is heard. The air is heavy with grief and something creeping.

Enter LADY CAPULET, disheveled, wrapped in a mourning veil. She walks with slow, mechanical steps. The NURSE is already present, sitting at Juliet's vanity table, holding a piece of Juliet's hair ribbon. Her eyes are sunken, her hands trembling.

LADY CAPULET (cold):

She was sixteen.
And now she is nothing.
Not a bride. Not a mother.
Only a corpse.

NURSE (quietly):

She was in love.

LADY CAPULET:

She was a child.

NURSE:

No... not at the end.

Lady Capulet turns sharply.

LADY CAPULET:

What are you saying?

NURSE:

I helped them.
I took her to him.
To Romeo.
I lied for her... I covered her steps.
I held the ladder as he climbed her balcony.
I made the marriage happen.

LADY CAPULET staggers back, as though struck.

LADY CAPULET:

You—
You traitorous—

She raises her hand but lets it drop.

LADY CAPULET:

You brought this plague upon us.

NURSE (sobbing):

I thought it was love!
She was so happy... she glowed like sunlight.
I thought it would save her.
But now she's cold.
She's stone.

She takes out a small vial from her sleeve.

NURSE (to herself):

She gave it to me.
A second vial—"for Romeo," she said.
In case he didn't get the message.
In case the world betrayed them.
She asked me to hold it—just in case.
Her hands tremble.

NURSE:

I kept it.
But maybe it was always meant for me

LADY CAPULET (horrified):

Don't you dare.

NURSE:

She trusted me with her life...
Now I'll follow her in death.

Before Lady Capulet can stop her, the NURSE drinks the poison. She falls forward into Juliet's vanity chair. Her head slumps onto the table.

LADY CAPULET:

No! No more!

She rushes to the body, too late. She lets out a raw, broken cry.

LADY CAPULET (screaming):

Juliet! Why did you take her too?

A sharp crash is heard outside the chamber. The windows flicker orange. Shouting grows louder.

VOICE (offstage, rioters):

Bring out the Capulets! Burn it down!
No more crowns! No more bloodlines!

Enter GUARD, wounded and panicked.

GUARD:

My lady—
The gates have fallen! They overran the west wall!

Another SCREAM is heard. Steel clashing. A second GUARD appears, then falls mid-step—stabbed in the back by a RIOTER charging in.

The RIOTER stares at Lady Capulet—bloodied, masked—and flees into the smoke without speaking.

LADY CAPULET (shaking):

Where are the gods now?

Flames begin to lick the floorboards near the curtains. The fire has reached the estate.

LADY CAPULET (last breath, barely audible):

Forgive me.

The fire consumes the frame. Screams vanish into crackling wood. The chamber collapses into ash and silence.

BLACKOUT.

Scene 3: The Collapse of Montague

Scene: The Montague estate. Once proud, now crumbling. The walls are cracked, windows broken. A faint orange glow flickers through the drapes—Verona is burning. LORD MONTAGUE sits alone in a high-backed chair, clutching a scroll. It's Romeo's exile order. His eyes are wide, glassy. A fireplace crackles nearby but does not warm the room.

Enter BENVOLIO, breathless, soot on his face, sword at his side.

BENVOLIO:

Uncle! The people are storming the outer walls—
They've breached the south gate. The Capulets are overrun.
The city is no longer ours.

LORD MONTAGUE doesn't respond. His fingers tighten around the scroll.

LADY MONTAGUE (hoarse):

They exiled him.
My son. My heir.
My Romeo.

BENVOLIO (urgently):

We must go—Lord Montague is preparing to flee.
We can still reach the friar's chapel—there's shelter underground.

LADY MONTAGUE slowly lifts his gaze to Benvolio.

LADY MONTAGUE:

There is no shelter from a name.
I spent my life defending Montague...
And it left my boy to die alone.

She tries to rise but falters. Benvolio catches her, steadying her in the chair.

BENVOLIO:

Then come—for his sake.
Live. Tell them who he truly was.

Enter LORD MONTAGUE, cloaked in dark linen, a travel satchel in hand. A RETAINER follows behind, clutching maps and provisions.

LORD MONTAGUE:

She won't move, will she?

Benvolio shakes his head.

LORD MONTAGUE (gently):

My love... we must go.

LADY MONTAGUE stares at him, then slowly lowers her head. Her breathing stills. The scroll slips from her hand.

BENVOLIO (alarmed):

My Lady!?

No response. Benvolio checks her pulse, then freezes.

BENVOLIO:

She's gone... Passed from a broken heart....

LORD Montague does not cry. He kneels beside his wife and closes her eyes.

LORD MONTAGUE (softly):

You followed him after all.

He rises, steadies himself, and hands Benvolio a folded cloth.

LORD MONTAGUE:

Take this. It's the last letter Romeo wrote.
It belongs in the crypt—with him.

BENVOLIO:

And you?

LORD MONTAGUE:

I go now... to bury the last of my house.

He nods to her retainer and exits silently. Benvolio turns to Lady Montague's chair—empty now—and picks up the scroll from the floor.

BENVOLIO (to himself):

Let the name die with dignity.
Romeo was more than Montague.

He draws his cloak and exits through the smoke-stained hallway. The firelight dances over the empty chair. A gust of wind scatters the ashes of the scroll across the floor.

BLACKOUT.

Scene 4: The Mob Devours Itself

Scene: Verona's merchant quarter. Once a place of trade and gossip, now a battleground. Torches burn in barrels. Debris blocks alleyways. Smoke drifts like fog. People scream offstage. The remnants of Capulet and Montague banners are trampled underfoot.

Enter TWO FACTIONS of the mob—some bearing Capulet colors, others Montague. Most wear makeshift armor, torn cloaks, bloodied tunics. Among them: CITIZENS, MOTHERS, YOUNG BOYS. None are trained soldiers—only survivors with blades.

FIRST MOB LEADER (Capulet side):

Down with the rats who spat on Tybalt's grave!

SECOND MOB LEADER (Montague side):

They lit the fire first! Their daughters brought death to us all!

CITIZEN (crying out):

No more names! No more houses!

YOUNG GIRL (clutching a doll):

Please—stop—

The mobs rush each other. Screams. Steel. Smoke. Chaos. Some drop weapons and run. Others keep fighting. Buildings burn in the background.

Enter a WOUNDED CAPULET GUARD, dragging a scorched Capulet banner.

WOUNDED GUARD:

They've killed Paris.
They've stormed the crypt.
The Capulet name is ash.

He collapses.

Enter an OLD MAN, ragged but unafraid, standing amidst the chaos. Her arms are raised. Her face is streaked with soot.

OLD MAN:

Stop! This is not your war! This was never your war!

A few hesitate. He steps forward.

OLD MAN (cont'd):

I sold him the poison. The Montague boy.
I gave him the death you all now feed on.

Gasps ripple through the crowd. The fighting slows—but only for a breath.

OLD MAN (cont'd):

You think your knives speak for justice?
You think your flames cleanse the grief?
You are not righteous. You are drowning in the blood of children.

But no one listens. Steel clashes again. The fire roars. The crowd resumes its slaughter.

A MOTHER shields her children under a broken cart. A CHILD holds a toy sword and watches the battle, silent.

The statue of Prince Escalus is pulled down in the background. It cracks against the stones.

The lights fade as the mob turns on itself—friend fighting friend, cousin stabbing cousin. Verona is devouring its own.

BLACKOUT.

ACT II

Embers of the Past

Scene 1: Beneath the Chapel

Scene: The crypt beneath Saint Verona. Quiet. Echoing. Two stone altars lie side by side, lit by candlelight. The bodies of ROMEO and JULIET rest atop them, dressed in white. Their faces are peaceful. Flowers are scattered across the floor—some wilted, some fresh. A censer swings slowly.

Enter FRIAR LAURENCE, cloaked in ash-stained robes. He kneels between the altars, speaking a prayer in low Latin. His hands shake. He lights another candle.

Footsteps echo in the stairwell.

Enter LORD MONTAGUE, hooded, his cloak soaked from travel. He moves carefully, clutching a small satchel. A RETAINER follows, carrying a lantern.

LORD MONTAGUE (softly):

This is where you brought them?

FRIAR LAURENCE (without turning):

Yes.

They rest together... at last.

He steps forward, her gaze fixed on Romeo. His breath catches. He kneels beside him, unable to speak for a moment.

LORD MONTAGUE:

I told him once he would break my heart.
He said it would never come to that.
But he did.
And with him, he took her.

FRIAR LAURENCE (quietly):

Lady Montague is gone?

LORD MONTAGUE:

Grief took her the moment they exiled our son.
She barely lived past the news.

He places a hand on Romeo's chest.

LORD MONTAGUE:

Now I am the last.

Another sound—slow, dragging steps.

Enter LORD CAPULET, wrapped in a cloak, wounded and barely upright. Two SERVANTS steady him. He limps toward the tombs and sees Juliet's face. He crumples to his knees beside her.

LORD CAPULET (barely audible):

My girl... my stubborn, laughing girl...

His hand touches hers. He weeps—silent, exhausted tears. Lord Montague looks at him, then down again. There is no hatred left.

LORD MONTAGUE (quietly):

She was so young.

LORD CAPULET:

She was fire.
Too bright for a world this cold.

LORD MONTAGUE:

I spent years teaching Romeo to hate your name.
And yet, here he is—beside her, even in death.

LORD CAPULET:

I promised her a future.
I gave her a tomb.

LORD MONTAGUE (sighs):

We did this.

LORD CAPULET:

No.
We inherited the match.
But we lit the fuse.

FRIAR LAURENCE (raising his hands):

Let all hatred end in this chamber.
Let no curse or name pass through these walls.
Here lies love.
And here... let it be buried.

He steps back and begins the funeral prayer.

FRIAR LAURENCE (prayer):

In life, they were torn.
In death, they are bound.
Let their peace bloom where our pride once reigned.
Let their silence speak for all we silenced.

Lord Montague turns to Lord Capulet to speak again—

LORD MONTAGUE:

They loved each other.
That was real.

LORD CAPULET (weakly):

I see that now.
It's all I see.

But Lord Capulet begins to slump. Lord Montague moves closer. His eyes are open but distant. He kneels and checks for breath.

LORD MONTAGUE:

He's gone.

Lord Montague places a single flower on Juliet's chest, one on Romeo's. He stands in silence for a moment, looking at the man he once hated.

LORD MONTAGUE (quietly):

My sworn enemy is dead...
and I feel no joy.
It feels as though I've lost a brother I never dared call friend.

He collects his satchel and walks toward the stair.

FRIAR LAURENCE:

Then let him rest with her.

FRIAR LAURENCE:

Where will you go?

LORD MONTAGUE:

Anywhere the fire hasn't touched yet.

He exits. The friar stands alone. The candles flicker.

He bows his head and begins snuffing the flames, one by one.

BLACKOUT.

Scene 2: Rosaline Among Ruins

Scene: A ruined courtyard near the old Capulet orchard. Weeds push through cracked marble. A bench sits beneath a lifeless tree. The statue of Venus has fallen and lies in pieces. Ash drifts across the stones. The world is quiet—but not at peace.

Enter ROSALINE, her cloak singed and torn. Her hair is unkempt, her eyes heavy. She carries a ribbon and a small stack of parchment, crumpled and stained. She walks slowly to the bench and sits. Her fingers run along the ribbon in silence.

ROSALINE (to herself):

He said he loved me.
Said the stars were dull beside my eyes.
He wrote me poems—dozens. Bad ones.

She lets out a bitter chuckle.

ROSALINE:

I told him no. Not yet.
Told him to try harder.
I thought I was being careful.
I wanted to be worth the effort.

She wipes at her face roughly, smearing ash across her cheek.

ROSALINE:

And then he saw her.
And forgot me like a name whispered in a dream.

She tosses the ribbon to the ground.

Enter FRIAR LAURENCE, carrying a lantern. He stops when he sees her.

FRIAR LAURENCE:

You survived.

ROSALINE (not turning):

I did.
Not sure if that was a kindness.

FRIAR LAURENCE:

I thought you had left Verona.

ROSALINE:

I did. And then I came back.
Where else can ghosts speak freely?

A pause.

FRIAR LAURENCE:

You mourn him.

ROSALINE:

I mourn what I thought I meant to him.
I mourn the girl who waited.
He didn't even say goodbye.

FRIAR LAURENCE:

He was young. He didn't know what he left behind.

ROSALINE (finally turning to him):

He knew enough to promise the stars.
He just didn't wait for the storm to pass.
Juliet was open. Soft. Immediate.
And I—I asked him to fight.
But he didn't want a challenge. He wanted a story.

She stands. Her voice hardens—not loud, but sharp.

ROSALINE:

So now I'm the discarded prologue.
The almost. The might-have-been.
And she's eternal, laid beside him in silk.

FRIAR LAURENCE:

They died for love.

ROSALINE:

No.
They died for pride. For haste.
For the thrill of being tragic.

She picks up one of the crumpled pages. Reads it aloud bitterly.

ROSALINE (reading):

"To Rosaline, whose silence is more lovely than speech."

She tears it in half.

ROSALINE:

I should've burned them all.
But I kept them.
Because I thought one day, he'd return.

She stares at the broken statue of Venus.

ROSALINE (softly):

I didn't want him to be a poem.
I wanted him to be real.
And stay.

She kneels and leaves the torn letter at the statue's base.

FRIAR LAURENCE:

Will you write your own version?

ROSALINE:

No.
I'll write the truth.

BLACKOUT.

Scene 3: The Last Montague

Scene: The remains of the Montague estate. The stone courtyard is cracked and covered in ash. Statues have fallen, the gates hang from their hinges. The fires are out, but the air is still smoky. Dawn is just beginning to rise in the east.

Enter BENVOLIO, cloaked and weary. He carries a small satchel and holds a sealed letter in one hand—Romeo's final words. His sword is broken. His eyes are sunken. He walks through the ruins slowly, as if saying goodbye to ghosts.

BENVOLIO (to himself):

I told him love would ruin us.
He laughed.
Said ruin was better than silence.

He stops at a shattered fountain—crimson-stained water pooled beneath its base. He drops to one knee beside it, exhausted.

BENVOLIO:

Mercutio bled out right here.
I held him.
Tried to joke with him—to lie for him.
He died laughing through the blood.
He always laughed.

He wipes his face. Ash and tears mix.

BENVOLIO:

And Romeo... he looked at Juliet like the sun finally answered him.
I watched him fall, fast and deep.
Then I watched him vanish.
To exile. To despair. To death.

He lays Romeo's letter on the fountain edge but doesn't open it.

BENVOLIO:

I tried. Gods know I tried.
To make peace. To slow the storm.
But no one listens to the quiet one.

He stands, unsteady.

BENVOLIO:

Now the names are ash.
The friends are ghosts.
And I am the last Montague.

He removes a strip of cloth from his belt—embroidered with the Montague crest.
He ties it around the broken spout, then steps back.

BENVOLIO:

Let this be the grave of our pride.
No statues. No songs.
Just the boy who stayed too long.

He turns to the city gates. The light of morning reaches the courtyard.

BENVOLIO:

I walk away not because I survived...
But because I lost everything.
No friends. No family. No cause.

He exits. The Montague crest flutters once in the breeze, then drops into the dust.

BLACKOUT.

Scene 4: The People Speak

Scene: The scorched edge of Verona's central square. Smoke rises from distant buildings. Broken tools and carts lie scattered. The once-lively market is quiet, except for a few CITIZENS standing in small clusters. Among them: a FISHMONGER, a MIDWIFE, a BLIND MAN, and the OLD MAN (the apothecary who sold the poison). They do not speak at first. The silence is thick.

FISHMONGER:

Three sons I raised. All gone. Not for war. Not for country. For names.

MIDWIFE:

I delivered Juliet. Held her when she first cried.
Now I've buried six babies in three days.

BLIND MAN:

I hear the bells at night. Not for prayer.
For death. For more bodies.
I keep count. I'm up to sixty-four.
A pause.

OLD MAN (stepping forward):

I gave the boy the poison.
My hands mixed the thing that took them both.
I told myself I was doing mercy.
But it was just business.
He paid me in gold. And now my shack is cinders. My coin melted in the fire.
All I bought was silence and ash.

A child runs across the square, dragging a wooden sword.

CHILD (shouting):

I'm a Capulet! No—I'm a Montague! Die, traitor!
The MIDWIFE grabs the child and pulls him close.

MIDWIFE (to child):

No more names.

FISHMONGER:

What do we call ourselves now?

BLIND MAN:

Survivors.

OLD MAN:

Ghosts.

A quiet falls. A breeze lifts ashes into the air. The people stare at the horizon, unsure whether to rebuild or run.

FISHMONGER:

The houses are dead.

MIDWIFE:

Then let something new be born.

BLACKOUT.

ACT III

Inferno

Scene 1: Fire in the House of Capulet

Scene: The once-grand Capulet estate. The roof is ablaze. Smoke coils through shattered windows. The night is red. The walls groan with heat. Inside the main hall, furniture is overturned, portraits blackened. The fire has breached the home of pride.

Enter LADY CAPULET, stumbling in from the garden. Her face is soot-streaked. She carries a silk shawl—the last thing she saved of Juliet's and a small silver hand mirror. Screams echo in the distance. Somewhere offstage, the crack of beams collapsing.

LADY CAPULET (to herself):

I gave her dolls carved from cedar.
Silk from Cyprus.
I raised her to walk with queens.
And now the house burns—and there are no daughters left to inherit it.

She touches a singed tapestry—one with the Capulet crest. It crumbles beneath her fingers.

Enter a YOUNG SERVANT, bleeding from the arm, breathless.

SERVANT:

My lady—we must go! They've breached the gate! The kitchens are gone—the chapel's in flames!

LADY CAPULET (still):

Let it burn.
Let every stone remember her name before it turns to ash.

The SERVANT tries to drag her toward the exit. She doesn't budge.

SERVANT:

Please—Juliet wouldn't want—
You must survive her!

LADY CAPULET (coldly):

I survived her once.
When she cried for love and I silenced her.
When I gave her a tomb instead of my arms.

She looks down at the shawl and the mirror. Slowly, she wraps the silver hand mirror inside the silk, as if preparing an offering.

The fire roars louder. The ceiling above them creaks.

LADY CAPULET:

Take this.
Her mirror—she used to hold it like a lantern.
Find the chapel.
If her body still lies there... lay this at her feet.
Tell her—her mother never stopped loving her.
Even when the world taught her not to say it.

The SERVANT takes it, stunned, holding it carefully.

SERVANT:

My lady... what of Lord Capulet?

Lady Capulet pauses—her voice trembling.

LADY CAPULET:

He's gone.
I feel it.
Like a shadow leaving the walls.
The fire roars louder. The ceiling above them creaks.

SERVANT (desperate):

If you stay, you'll die!

LADY CAPULET:

Then let it be beside her.
A Capulet to the end.

She turns her back to the servant. Her steps are steady now—measured. She steps forward, into the red glow of the collapsing stairs. The SERVANT watches in horror as she disappears beyond the smoke.

A sudden CRASH. A beam falls. The flames rise. The SERVANT clutches the wrapped mirror to his chest and flees into the dark.

BLACKOUT.

Scene 2: The Night Funeral

Scene: A stone crypt beneath the ruined chapel. The air is thick with incense and smoke. Two stone biers hold the bodies of ROMEO and JULIET, side by side, dressed in white. Their hands are gently clasped together. Candles flicker. Dust settles in the corners.

Enter FRIAR LAURENCE, alone. He carries a single candle, walking with care. He stands before the bodies, silent.

FRIAR LAURENCE (whispers):

I gave them a promise.
That love would endure...
And in death, it has.

He places white flowers at their feet.

*Enter **LORD MONTAGUE**, cloaked in black. He walks to Romeo and kneels beside him.*

LORD MONTAGUE:

I told you to be careful.
I told you not to chase shadows.
But you followed your heart—into the grave.

He places a ring beside his son's hand.

LORD MONTAGUE:

Your mother died with your name on her lips.
I'll carry the rest in silence.

Enter BALTHASAR, carrying a cloth-wrapped bundle. He approaches quietly.

BALTHASAR:

My lord.
I followed him from Mantua.
I brought... this.

He unwraps Romeo's dagger and places it beside the body.

BALTHASAR (softly):

Forgive me, master.

He steps back into the shadows.

Enter a YOUNG SERVANT, burned at the sleeve, limping, eyes wide with grief. He carries a half-charred silver hand mirror, wrapped in torn silk. He approaches Juliet slowly and kneels.

YOUNG SERVANT:

This was her mother's.
She kept it by her bedside.
When the house caught fire...
Lady Capulet gave it to me.
She said, "Lay it at her feet."
She didn't make it out either.

He gently unwraps the bundle and places the scorched mirror beside Juliet.

YOUNG SERVANT (voice breaking):

She died calling your name.
He kneels quietly beside Juliet, hands folded.

ROSALINE enters, silent, standing near the entrance. She watches the mourners, the grief suspended in candlelight. After a long moment, she steps forward.

She kneels between the two biers, lays a hand gently on Juliet's wrist, then Romeo's. Her voice is soft but certain.

ROSALINE:

They burned for love.
They bled for pride.
And now, they rest—together.
No prince. No father. No feud can touch them here.

She looks at each of the offerings left—dagger, ring, mirror. She takes a scrap of parchment from her sleeve and sets it beside Juliet's hand.

ROSALINE:

This is my vow.
To tell the truth of them.
Not the pretty version.
Not the lie Verona needs to feel clean.
But what really happened.
Because if we forget... we repeat.

She stands, turning to the others, her voice steady.

She got the ending.

Now I'll write the rest.

FRIAR LAURENCE (softly):

Let all that remains of hatred end in this chamber.
Let the names dissolve—stone to dust.
What they could not be in life,
Let them be in memory:
Whole.

A candle flickers out. The wind moves faintly through the crypt.

GUARD (offstage):

By order of the Prince—
Lord Montague is to be held until the council rules.

Lord Montague looks up—tired, unresisting. He lowers his head as the guards escort him out. No protest. No drama. Just the quiet weight of consequence.

BLACKOUT.

Scene 3: The Confession

Scene: The crypt, later that same night. The candles have burned lower. Only a few flicker now. The others are melted stubs, puddled around the base of the tombs. JULIET and ROMEO remain untouched. Silence reigns.

Enter FRIAR LAURENCE slowly, carrying a parchment and ink. His robes are stained with ash and his hands tremble. He kneels at a small stone table set near the back of the crypt.

FRIAR LAURENCE (to himself):

What use is confession when the world no longer listens?

He unrolls the parchment and begins to write. His voice speaks aloud the words he puts to paper.

FRIAR LAURENCE (writing):

"To whoever finds this letter:
I, Laurence of Verona, write this not as a priest,
but as the man who watched two children die beneath the weight of names not their own."
\n
"I wed them in secret.
I counseled their deceit.
I gave her the draught that made her still,
and failed to deliver the message that could have saved them both."
\n

"I believed love would save us.
I was wrong."

He sets the quill down and stands. The robe falls heavier now on his shoulders.

He walks to Juliet's bier, places the letter beneath her hand, then stands before both bodies.

FRIAR LAURENCE:

I tried to build peace from lies.
And so the truth buried us all.

He unties the rope belt from around his waist. One by one, he removes his robe and lays it folded at the foot of the altar. Beneath it, simple clothes: not a priest, but a man.

FRIAR LAURENCE:

I am no shepherd.
I am only another sinner.

He takes one last look at the tombs.

FRIAR LAURENCE (softly):

Let the dead forgive me.

He walks slowly toward the exit, the wind curling through the doorway. His steps echo as the last candle gutter-flames behind him.

BLACKOUT.

Scene 4: Too Late

Scene: The crypt, just before dawn. A single candle burns low near the feet of ROMEO and JULIET. The air is still. The folded priest's robe lies untouched near the altar. The letter remains beneath Juliet's hand.

Enter FRIAR JOHN, breathing heavily, clothes rumpled, his sandals muddy. He stumbles down the crypt steps, calling softly.

FRIAR JOHN:

Laurence?
Brother?

He stops when he sees the bodies. He approaches slowly, trembling. His eyes fall on the robe, then the letter. He reads it—silently at first, then aloud, breaking as he goes.

FRIAR JOHN (reading):

"...I wed them in secret.
I gave her the draught... and failed to deliver the message."

He drops the letter. His voice cracks.

FRIAR JOHN:

I was locked in. A plague wall. No one could leave Mantua.

He kneels beside Romeo.

FRIAR JOHN:

I tried. By God, I tried.

He looks around. His gaze falls on the communal wine left behind on the friar's stone table. He stumbles over to it. Uncorks it. Stares.

FRIAR JOHN:

What use is salvation... when the grave keeps no record of intentions?

He drinks—once, deeply. Again. He sinks down beside the wall, the bottle clutched in one hand, his breathing uneven.

FRIAR JOHN (slurring):

I should've run faster.
I should've screamed louder.
But the city chose silence.
And I... I obeyed.

He drinks again. Then rises unsteadily, clutching the bottle. He walks to the doorway and looks back once—at the robe, the letter, the dead.

FRIAR JOHN (murmuring):

No sermons left.
Only silence.

He gently rolls the scroll and slips it into his robe. He takes one last swig from the wine flask.

He exits into the dark. The candle sputters out.

BLACKOUT.

ACT IV

ACT IV

Ashes of Verona

Scene 1: The Telling

Scene: The Verona marketplace, now mostly rubble. The stalls are charred, banners fallen, and ash lays like dust over every surface. A fire smolders in a barrel nearby. There are no soldiers, no banners—just survivors. The MIDWIFE, the OLD MAN (apothecary), the FISHMONGER, and the CHILD stand scattered among others.

Enter ROSALINE, carrying a satchel filled with scrolls. Her clothes are plain. She walks to a broken merchant's platform and steps atop it. She faces the people—not to inspire, but to speak truth.

ROSALINE:

You've heard the story already.
Two children, torn by love.
Two names, heavier than blood.
But what they lived—what they died for—was not romance.
It was silence.
And silence is the cruelest killer of all.

The CITIZENS listen. Even the fire seems to quiet. She unrolls a page, creased and rewritten many times.

ROSALINE:

They were not saints.
They were not symbols.
They were children.
And every one of us let them die.

A pause. She looks to the CHILD standing nearby.

ROSALINE (to the child):

Take this. Copy it. Tell it.
Not as a poem. Not as a fairytale.
As truth.
So they are never forgotten.
So no one dares to repeat this.

She hands the child the scroll. He kneels, begins transcribing onto a fresh parchment.

Around them, people begin sweeping ash, clearing rubble—quietly, slowly. A WOMAN drops two scorched helmets into the fire. The MIDWIFE takes a burnt crest and tosses it in as well.

At the edge of the square, CITIZENS pile bodies—burnt, bloodied, broken. Capulet. Montague. Servant. Noble. No names now. Just the dead. They cover them with tattered sheets, one by one, in silence.

FISHMONGER:

No Montagues. No Capulets.
Just us.

OLD MAN (sharply):

Just what's left...
...while the Prince dines behind guarded gates.

MIDWIFE (bitter):

He drank their wine. Took their gifts.
Watched the city burn from a tower window.

FISHMONGER:

And now he sends no guards. No word.

CHILD (softly):

Who rules us now?

MIDWIFE (without hesitation):

No one.
Not until we choose better.

OLD MAN (quietly, but firm):

No more lords who sell silence for coin.

ROSALINE (gazing across the square):

Then let today be the day it ends.
No names. No crowns.

Just truth.

The child continues writing. The sun rises over the broken city. A bell tolls once. The breeze scatters ash across the market. The scroll in the boy's hand flutters with a breath of new beginning.

BLACKOUT.

Scene 2: The Letter

Scene: A quiet alley behind the ruins of the chapel. The sky is still gray with ash. Morning is breaking. FRIAR JOHN slumps against a wall, bottle of wine nearly empty beside him. He mutters in half-sleep.

Enter ROSALINE, cautious. She stops when she sees him, frowns, and approaches.

ROSALINE:

You were meant to carry a letter.

FRIAR JOHN (groggy, ashamed):

I... I couldn't. They locked the gates. Mantua was quarantined... I tried—

ROSALINE (interrupting):

Trying didn't save them.

She kneels beside him. He pulls the folded confession from his coat and offers it without a word. She takes it.

Rosaline opens the letter and reads it in silence. Her expression flickers—shock, pain, clarity.

ROSALINE (quietly):

This is the truth.

She looks at the broken man beside her, then at the sky, then down at the letter again.

ROSALINE:

They'll call it love. They'll call it destiny.
But I will call it what it was: failure.
Pride. Silence. Fear.

She folds the letter and places it in her satchel. Stands tall.

ROSALINE:

Let the myth die.
Let the truth live.

She turns to walk away, then stops and looks back.

ROSALINE (softly):

What's your name?

FRIAR JOHN:

John.

ROSALINE:

Then go, John. Find your penance. Or let it find you.

He nods slowly, unable to speak. She exits the alley, her silhouette swallowed by the light of morning.

Friar John finishes the last sip of wine. He watches the bottle for a moment, then sets it down gently. He looks toward the chapel, then away—choosing not to return.

Offstage, a bell rings again. This time not for mourning—but for beginning.

BLACKOUT.

Scene 3: The Monument

Scene: The outskirts of Verona. A quiet hill overlooking the city. A simple stone monument stands at the center—newly placed. It bears no names, only an inscription: "To those who burned, and those who tried to love."

Enter the CHILD from the marketplace, carrying a small bundle of scrolls. Behind him, a few CITIZENS: the MIDWIFE, the FISHMONGER, the OLD MAN. Rosaline watches from a distance.

CHILD (softly):

They were wrong.
This wasn't just about them.
It was about all of us.

The CHILD kneels and places the scrolls beneath the stone.

The MIDWIFE lays a dried lavender sprig.

The OLD MAN lights a candle.

The FISHMONGER leaves a scale once used at Capulet feasts.

Others add ribbons, pages, stones—each an offering.

ROSALINE *watches from a distance, then slowly approaches.*

ROSALINE:

We came here to remember them.
But remembering is not enough.
Not anymore.

She looks back toward the broken city in the distance.

ROSALINE:

Meet me at the square.
There's something they all must hear.

DISSOLVE TO:

Cut to the city square. The people gather—not as Montagues or Capulets—but as a city. ROSALINE stands on the broken platform again. She unrolls Friar Laurence's letter and begins to read.

ROSALINE:

"This is not a tale of star-crossed lovers.
It is a confession.
Of choices made in fear.
Of silence mistaken for peace.
Of a city that let its children die."

The crowd listens in silence—no outrage, no protest. Only understanding. Heads bow. Some weep. Others stand straighter, as if finally seeing the weight of what was lost.

When she finishes, ROSALINE folds the letter. The CHILD approaches and offers her his version of the story—carefully written, neat, bound with a strip of blue ribbon.

CHILD:

This one... I made it true.

She takes it gently. Nods. places both scrolls beneath the edge of the broken platform.

ROSALINE:

Then maybe Verona has a chance.
The crowd responds—not with cheers, but with a quiet murmur.

CROWD (softly, overlapping):

Never again.
Not with our children.
Not in our name.

A breeze moves through the square.
The scent is not of ash—
But of soil.
Of spring.

BLACKOUT.

Scene 4: A Quiet Vow

Scene: Early morning. Smoke still lingers faintly in the air. Rosaline walks through the scorched remains of the Capulet chapel. A few nuns clear rubble and plant herbs among the cracked stones where a courtyard once stood.

Rosaline wears a simple cloak. Her steps are quiet, her face unreadable. One nun glances up, recognizing her—but says nothing. Rosaline pauses before the altar, where the statue of the Virgin leans cracked and blackened.

Footsteps behind her.

*Enter the **PRINCE**, flanked by two guards. He is older now, haggard. One sleeve of his robe is torn. His hands are stained with ink and ash.*

PRINCE:

You all vanish, one by one.
The lovers. The fathers. The firebrands.
And now you too?

Rosaline does not turn.

PRINCE (bitterly):

The city groans. Its bones are broken.
And you'd rather wear robes than rebuild it?

ROSALINE (still facing forward):

You had your chance to mend it—when it mattered.
Now you write new laws on old blood.

PRINCE:

You think silence makes you pure?

ROSALINE:

No. It makes me finished.

PRINCE:

And truth?

ROSALINE:

Truth is what's left after the shouting stops.
I've left it behind—written, not spoken.

She steps to the base of the altar and kneels in the ash where Juliet once stood.
She removes her ring and places it beside the soot-covered statue of the Virgin.

ROSALINE (to herself):

No more names.
No more sides.

*She rises and turns to the **Mother Superior**, who nods. No ceremony. No blessing. Only a glance.*

Rosaline walks toward the cloister garden. As she vanishes behind the veil of morning, her voice fades.

ROSALINE (softly):

Let Verona bury me too.

*The **Prince** watches her go. He does not stop her. His hands tremble.*

PRINCE (to his guards):

She chooses silence.
Like the rest of them.

He turns and leaves. No salute. No decree. Just footsteps over stone.

A bell tolls once. A vow is sealed.

ACT V

ACT V

Ghosts of Verona

Scene 1: The Orchard

Scene: A quiet orchard overlooking Verona. Morning light cuts through the trees. A soft breeze stirs the leaves. The city below is calm.

Enter the BOY, now a young man, dressed in simple scholar's robes. He carries a worn notebook and a satchel. He approaches a stone marked "R + J."

BOY (to himself): So many names carved in fire. And only two remembered in love.

He kneels by the stone and removes a bound manuscript. He sets it down gently.

BOY: This is for them. For all of them.

He steps back. The wind rustles the pages. He turns to leave, pausing once to look back.

Enter the ghostly figures of ROMEO and JULIET. They walk hand-in-hand, silent. They stand over the manuscript, reading without words. They look out over Verona.

A gentle light grows behind them—sunrise. The orchard glows gold.

The BOY watches from the edge, then quietly exits.

NARRATION (voiceover): Time passed, and the tale remained. The boy became a man. A writer. He took a new name—Luigi da Porto. And one day, a poet would read his story...

BLACKOUT.

EPILOGUE

Epilogue

Scene: A small study lit by candlelight, years later. Shelves of books line the walls. A desk sits at the center, scattered with quills, open scrolls, and a single faded blue ribbon.

A YOUNG SCHOLAR (the CHILD, now older) sits at the desk, carefully transcribing a manuscript. His writing is calm, deliberate. A finished page bears the title: "The Fall of Two Houses."

He sets his quill down and looks out the window. The bells of Verona ring in the distance—not for mourning, but for daily life. Outside, the square is bustling with new market stalls, laughter, children chasing one another. Peace has returned, though not without cost.

He thinks of Rosaline, who kept her vow and was never seen again outside the convent walls.

He recalls the Prince, who ruled just long enough to rebuild the square—then passed his seal to a council formed from among the people.

He thinks softly of Benvolio, who vanished into the countryside and was never seen again, but whose name was carved into a chapel bench by a lonely traveler.

He remembers the young servant who brought Juliet's heirloom. No one knows what became of him, though some say he wandered far and joined the Brothers in gray.

Lord Montague was tried—not for murder, but for silence. They said he taught Romeo to hate and then blamed the boy for learning.

No one knows what became of John, only that he never served as friar again.

And then he pauses, placing his hand gently on the bound story on his desk.

SCHOLAR: They were not the last to die for pride, nor the first to love without permission. But they will be remembered—not as legend, but as warning.

SCHOLAR (to himself):

They burned for love.

They bled for pride.

And we—

We remember so we do not repeat.

He walks to a nearby shelf and places the sealed manuscript beside several others—each a different story of Verona, bound in faded cloth and leather. History preserved not in marble, but in memory.

He returns to the desk, draws out a small wooden box, and opens it to reveal a locket with a miniature sketch—Romeo and Juliet, hand in hand beneath a tree. He looks at it for a long moment.

A knock at the door. A NEW CHILD stands, wide-eyed, cradling a blank journal.

NEW CHILD:

Is it true? Did it all really happen?

SCHOLAR (smiling faintly):

Sit down.

I'll tell you the real story.
One day, someone else will write it again—maybe under a different name.
A poet. A playwright. Someone who still believes words can save us.
But I was there.
I was Luigi da Porto.

The candlelight flickers. The scholar begins to speak, and the quill begins to scratch. Offstage, a distant voice—soft, like a whisper across centuries—recites the opening of "Romeo and Juliet."

Two households, both alike in dignity,

In fair Verona, where we lay our scene,

From ancient grudge break to new mutiny,

Where civil blood makes civil hands unclean....

BLACKOUT.

Let Verona rest.

Fin

Reader's Guide

(For Classrooms, Book Clubs, or Talkbacks)

Discussion Questions:

1. Rosaline begins the play as a forgotten figure and ends as a silent witness.

How does her journey reflect the emotional cost of survival?
Does her silence become a source of power—or of pain?

2. The play explores how truth and myth often conflict.

By the end, who controls the narrative of Romeo and Juliet's legacy?
Is preserving a painful truth more important than allowing a beautiful lie to endure?

3. Benvolio is the last Montague to walk away.

What does his departure reveal about the burden of legacy and the isolation of survival?
Does he represent peace—or abandonment?

4. Lord Montague is arrested not for violence, but for silence.

Is his punishment justified?
What does this suggest about guilt, complicity, and generational responsibility?

5. The title The Fall of Two Houses implies more than the death of families.

What else collapses in this play—ideals, power, traditions?
And what rises in their place?

6. What role does memory play in this story?

How do different characters preserve, distort, or bury the past—and why does that matter?

7. Is Friar Laurence a villain, a coward, or just a flawed human being?

What does the play suggest about those who do too little, too late?

8. The child becomes both a scribe and a symbol of the future.

How does their presence reframe the tragedy?
What does the play say about who gets to tell history—and who is erased from it?

www.ingramcontent.com/pod-product-compliance
Lightning Source LLC
Chambersburg PA
CBHW061701120626
46550CB00003B/1041